T0065748

FISHERMAN
BIBLE STUDYGUIDES

Women at Midlife

EMBRACING THE CHALLENGES

BY JEANIE MILEY

SHAW

WATERBROOK
PRESS

Women at Midlife

A SHAW BOOK
PUBLISHED BY WATERBROOK PRESS
2375 Telstar Drive, Suite 160
Colorado Springs, Colorado 80920
A division of Random House, Inc.

ISBN-13: 978-0-877-88858-1

Printed in the United States of America
2001

Contents

Welcome to the Women of the Word Series

BY RUTH HALEY BARTON

elcome to the Women of the Word studyguides—a series especially designed to encourage women in their spiritual journey. No matter what season of life we may be in or how long we have followed Christ, we all face similar issues as women in today's world. Discovering who we are, living in relationship with others, choosing a vocational path, satisfying our spiritual hunger—we women face an unprecedented array of options. At times we are exhilarated by the opportunities, running enthusiastically from option to option like shoppers in a brand-new superstore. At other times we are confused and desperate for guidance—almost paralyzed by a panoply of choices far beyond what women in previous generations could have imagined. We need wisdom that speaks to the complexity of our lives.

Perhaps even deeper than our need for "answers" to life's questions is the desire for an intimate encounter with God. We long for a fresh expression of God's loving concern for us, a sense of personal attention in the midst of an alarmingly impersonal world. And so we approach the Scriptures with high hopes. We know that the Bible is a book like no other— God-breathed not only at the time of its initial writing but also alive and active in the present moment (Hebrews 4:12). Yet we're not always sure how to access it for ourselves. We might wonder, "Will I really have a life-giving encounter with God through the words on these pages, or is that a privilege reserved for others? How do *I* receive the life-changing power that is present in this ancient text?"

One concrete and effective way to open ourselves up to God's work in our lives is through inductive Bible study. This approach involves a dynamic interplay between the mind and the heart. First we engage our minds to read and unravel the meaning of the text. Through careful study and thought, we consider the historical context, explore the meaning of words, concepts, and principles, and reflect on what these might have meant to the original listeners. But the task of observing and interpreting information about the text is just the beginning. It is the "front porch" that leads into the "main house" of our relationship with God. No matter how nice a front porch is, we don't want to stay there forever. We want to be invited to come inside, to get comfortable, to share food and fellowship with the Master of the house. Inductive Bible study offers us just such an invitation—to engage not only our minds but also our hearts as we listen for God's Word for us today.

Our spiritual companions on this journey include the ancient women of the Bible, whose lives bear striking similarities to our own: single women making choices about relationships and lifestyle; young mothers trying to figure out how to balance love for children with other life callings; married women wrestling with the joys and the challenges of long-term commitment; women learning how to answer God's call to service and leadership in the church, the marketplace, and the global community. Regardless of differences in historical and cultural settings, their experiences and life lessons, their successes and failures speak powerfully to our own. Like us, they harbored deep and perhaps inexpressible desires for a life-transforming connection with God. Their lives demonstrate that the God who cared for a slave girl and her baby in the wilderness, answered an infertile woman's prayer, granted wisdom, political savvy, and protection to a Hebrew beauty queen, and extended loving, human touch to women who had looked for love in all the wrong places is the same God who reaches for relationship with us today.

All Scripture, including the stories of those women who have gone before, is given for our instruction, inspiration, and spiritual formation (2 Timothy 3:16). The Women of the Word studyguide series offers you a powerful tool for engaging the Scriptures for spiritual transformation. As you embark on this study, I encourage you to engage your *mind* by being disciplined in your study of historical context, biblical language, and concepts through the notes provided and other trustworthy study materials that you might have on hand. I also encourage you to engage your *imagination* as you reflect on what the biblical teachings might have meant to the women who first heard them. But don't stop there! Take the most courageous step of all by engaging your *heart* and making it your top priority to listen for *God's word to you* in the present moment.

Each time you open God's Word begin with a quiet prayer: "Speak, Lord, for your servant is listening." Trust that he will speak and then, when he does, listen and respond with increasing faithfulness so that you become a woman whose life and character are shaped by the Word.

How to Use This Studyguide

*F*isherman studyguides are based on the inductive approach to Bible study. Inductive study is discovery study; we discover what the Bible says as we ask questions about its content and search for answers. This is quite different from the process in which a teacher *tells* a group *about* the Bible—what it means and what to do about it. In inductive study God speaks directly to each of us through his Word.

A group functions best when a leader keeps the discussion on target, but the leader is neither the teacher nor the "answer person." A leader's responsibility is to *ask*—not *tell*. The answers come from the text itself as group members examine, discuss, and think together about the passage.

There are four kinds of questions in each study. The first is an *approach question*. Asked and answered before the Bible passage is read, this question breaks the ice and helps you start thinking about the topic of the Bible study. It begins to reveal where thoughts and feelings need to be transformed by Scripture.

Some of the early questions in each study are *observation questions*—who, what, where, when, and how—designed to help you learn some basic facts about the passage of Scripture.

Once you know what the Bible says, you then need to ask, *What does it mean?* These *interpretation questions* help you to discover the writer's basic message.

Next come *application questions,* which ask, *What does it mean to me?* They challenge you to live out the Scripture's life-transforming message.

Fisherman studyguides provide spaces between questions for jotting down responses as well as any related questions you would like to raise in the group. Each group member should have a copy of the studyguide and may take a turn in leading the group.

A group should use any accurate, modern translation of the Bible such as the *New International Version,* the *New American Standard Bible,* the *New Revised Standard Version,* the *New Jerusalem Bible,* or the *Good News Bible.* (Other translations or paraphrases of the Bible may be referred to when additional help is needed.) Bible commentaries should not be brought to a Bible study because they tend to dampen discussion and keep people from thinking for themselves.

Suggestions for Group Leaders

1. Thoroughly read and study the Bible passage before the meeting. Get a firm grasp on its themes and begin applying its teachings for yourself. Pray that the Holy Spirit will "guide you into all truth" (John 16:13) so that your leadership will guide others.

2. If any of the studyguide's questions seem ambiguous or unnatural to you, rephrase them, feeling free to add others that seem necessary to bring out the meaning of a verse.

3. Begin (and end) the study promptly. Start by asking someone to pray for every participant to both understand the passage and be open to its transforming power. Remember, the Holy Spirit is the teacher, not you!

4. Ask for volunteers to read the passages aloud.

5. As you ask the studyguide's questions in sequence, encourage everyone to participate in the discussion. If some are silent, try gently suggesting, "Let's have an answer from someone who hasn't spoken up yet."

6. If a question comes up that you can't answer, don't be afraid to admit that you're baffled. Assign the topic as a research project for someone to report on next week, or say, "I'll do some studying and let you know what I find out."

7. Keep the discussion moving, but be sure it stays focused. Though a certain number of tangents are inevitable, you'll want to quickly bring the discussion back to the topic at hand. Also, learn to pace the discussion so that you finish the lesson in the time allotted.

8. Don't be afraid of silences; some questions take time to answer and some people need time to gather courage to speak. If silence persists, rephrase your question, but resist the temptation to answer it yourself.

9. If someone comes up with an answer that is clearly illogical or unbiblical, ask her for further clarification: "What verse suggests that to you?"

10. Discourage overuse of cross-references. Learn all you can from the passage at hand, while selectively incorporating a few important references suggested in the studyguide.

11. Some questions are marked with a ⮱. This indicates that further information is available in the Leader's Notes at the back of the guide.

12. For further information on getting a new Bible
    study group started and keeping it functioning
    effectively, read Gladys Hunt's *You Can Start a Bible
    Study Group* and *Pilgrims in Progress: Growing
    through Groups* by Jim and Carol Plueddemann
    (both available from Shaw Books).

Suggestions for Group Members

1. Learn and apply the following ground rules for
   effective Bible study. (If new members join the
   group later, review these guidelines with the whole
   group.)
2. Remember that your goal is to learn all that you can
   from the Bible passage being studied. Let it speak for
   itself without using Bible commentaries or other
   Bible passages. There is more than enough in each
   assigned passage to keep your group productively
   occupied for one session. Sticking to the passage
   saves the group from insecurity ("I don't have the
   right reference books—or the time to read anything
   else.") and confusion ("Where did that come from?
   I thought we were studying _____.").
3. Avoid the temptation to bring up those fascinating
   tangents that don't really grow out of the passage
   you are discussing. If the topic is of common interest, you can bring it up later in informal conversa-
   tion after the study. Meanwhile, help one another
   stick to the subject.
4. Encourage one another to participate. People remember best what they discover and verbalize for

themselves. Some people are naturally shy, while others may be afraid of making a mistake. If your discussion is free and friendly and you show real interest in what group members think and feel, the quieter ones will be more likely to speak up. Remember, the more people involved in a discussion, the richer it will be.

5. Guard yourself from answering too many questions or talking too much. Give others a chance to share their ideas. If you are one who participates easily, discipline yourself by counting to ten before you open your mouth!

6. Make personal, honest applications and commit yourself to letting God's Word change you.

Women at Midlife

*M*idlife. If you're there, you know that it's a season of changes, some welcome and some not. Relationships and responsibilities are changing as children leave home and older family members require increasing care or die. Work and career options are narrowing for some. For others, the second half of life provides incredibly rich freedom and new opportunities. Midlife is a major transition time in our lives as we learn to live with consequences of past choices and make new choices for the future. Midlife is about both what happens to us and what we make happen.

While the Bible may not address the specific issues that we women face throughout a lifetime, it does give principles and guidance for dealing with tough times—midlife included. God's Word teaches us how to grieve things we have lost and press on into the future. It provides comfort and challenge to those who have lost their way and forgiveness for those living with regrets. It offers a vision to those who are willing to walk boldly and confidently into the future, trusting in the provision, protection, and power of the Creator who holds all things in his hands.

Throughout my own midlife transition, I floundered and flailed until I realized that the God who made me still had a plan for me. He was still at work, leading me out of what had been rich and rewarding, fulfilling and wonderful, into a new era of freedom and fun, productivity and purpose. In order to move with grace into the next chapter of my life, I had to assess where I had been, let go of what was no longer to be, and find a new vision for this new time in my life.

My purpose in writing this studyguide is to encourage women facing the midlife transition to tap into the wellspring of possibility and promise that God offers us in Scripture. The truths we find there will give us stability for riding the rapids of change. As you go through this guide, place your own life story up against the grand story of God's infinite care and purpose for your life. Work the truths you discover into your everyday life, kneading them like yeast into the realities of work and play, relationships and difficulties. Trying to live what you learn will help you move on and out into wider spaces of God's grace.

My prayer is that the Scripture passages here will become fresh and vibrant and alive with meaning for you and that you will choose life and liberty in these coming years—years that can be your most fulfilling, rewarding, joyous, and loving. And may you make this journey with the confidence that you are a much-loved child of God.

For I am the LORD, your God, who takes hold
of your right hand and says to you,
Do not fear; I will help you.
ISAIAH 41:13

Remembering Who Made Me

PSALM 139:1-16,23-24

"*I* don't even feel like the same person anymore!" Joan lamented to her friend on her forty-fifth birthday. "It's as if everything is changing all around me, and I don't know the rules anymore. Is this a midlife crisis?"

Perhaps you can relate to those words. Midlife can be an unsettling time. But it also provides a perfect opportunity for us to reassess our relationship with God. It is a time to turn to the unchanging nature of God who is present, available, and actively involved in the highs and lows, the ups and downs of life. Throughout the centuries, people in trouble and transition have turned to the psalms to reorient and steady themselves. Psalm 139 reminds us to look at the big picture of the sovereignty of God in our lives.

1. When you hear the term "midlife crisis," what comes to your mind?

READ PSALM 139:1-16.

2. What details does the psalmist's prayer give us about God's intimate knowledge of our daily lives (verses 1-5)?

3. Note the various verbs used in verses 1-5. What do these actions tell us about God?

4. How does the psalmist respond to this knowledge (verse 6)? What is your response?

5. Is there any place God cannot go with you? Explain.

How does the assurance of God's constant watching over you help as you go through the changes of midlife?

6. The psalmist refers to darkness in verses 11-12. How can midlife seem like a kind of darkness?

7. In what ways has God been involved in your life from the very beginning (verses 13-16)?

What does verse 16 indicate about the continuing purpose and meaning of your life?

8. Describe the ways this psalm can help a person who is struggling with loneliness at midlife.

Read Psalm 139:23-24.

9. Compare and contrast these closing verses with the opening verses of the psalm.

✎10. What "anxious thoughts" or "offensive way[s]" do you think God may be calling you to release?

What would be the benefits of letting these go at this point in your life?

Life Changes

11. Many women come to midlife having shaped their schedules according to the needs of others. What does this psalm have to say about the sacredness of your own unique life?

12. What difference does it make to remember that God is your Maker and that he designed you? Pray together that these truths will become the foundation of this new phase of your life.

Remembering Who I Am

Isaiah 43:1-7; Psalm 8

*F*riend, sister, wife, mother, employee, employer, cook, chauffeur… It's amazing to consider the variety of skills women have acquired to get themselves and others through life. If I had known all the changing roles and twists and turns in the journey of adulthood, I'm not sure I would have had the courage to face the challenges. And in the midst of all that, it's all too easy to lose sight of who we are.

The children of Israel experienced many twists and turns in their national identity as well. Even in the midst of their troubles and spiritual decay, God's loving, seeking heart cried out through the prophet Isaiah's call for repentance and renewal. The story of Israel reminds us that God continues to call us back home to his heart and to assure us that we are his.

1. As you think back over the past week, how many "hats" did you wear? How many different roles did you fill?

READ ISAIAH 43:1-7.

2. Who is speaking? How does the speaker identify himself throughout this passage?

3. What are the repeated phrases and/or themes in this passage?

What ultimate assurance does God give to his people?

4. What general facts about Israel's history can you
    gather from the references in verses 3-6?

    In light of this, why would God's words of assurance
    be important to the children of Israel?

5. In what way is the imagery in verse 2 appropriate
    for some of the experiences of midlife?

    Why is turning to God the best response to difficulty?

6. Think back to your answer to question 1. What difference does it make to realize that God knows you by name (verse 1)?

READ PSALM 8.

7. What is significant about the way the psalmist begins and ends his song?

8. What question is at the heart of this psalm of praise?

9. How do human beings fit in with the rest of God's creation (verses 4-8)?

What does this say about the value God places on human life?

10. What have you learned from both of these passages about who you are?

What have you learned about who God is?

Life Changes

11. One day all of your roles and responsibilities will come to an end, but one part of your identity will never change: *You are a much-loved child of God.* What difference does this truth make as you face the choices and changes of midlife?

12. Perhaps you have friends who are at the same point in life. How can you spread the good news of God's love to others who may be clinging to their roles of the past in hopes of retaining a sense of identity and significance?

Letting Go and Handling Loss

LUKE 24:13-35; ISAIAH 43:18-19

Try to imagine what it might have been like for Jesus' followers in the dark days following his crucifixion. Perhaps someone sneered, "He wasn't all you thought he was, was he? What are you going to do now?" "I know you are going to miss him," another person might have said, "but you've got to get on with your life."

It must have been difficult for the disciples to answer the skeptics' questions after Jesus died a criminal's death on a cross. Their dreams seemed dashed upon the rocks of failure and disgrace. In this study we will travel for a while with two of Jesus' followers and see what God does at a particularly hard time in their lives.

1. What, for you, is one of the hardest parts about letting go of someone or something you love?

READ LUKE 24:13-35.

2. Who are these travelers and why have they left Jerusalem?

3. What is significant about the day on which they were traveling to Emmaus (verses 13,21)?

4. What have these disciples lost? Who had they believed Jesus to be (verses 19-21)?

How are they dealing with their disappointment (verses 14-18)?

5. Why do you think they don't recognize Jesus (verse 16)?

What difference does Jesus' appearance (though unknown) make to them at this point in their journey?

6. Do you think Jesus is aware of their grief? Explain.

In what specific ways does Jesus comfort the travelers and give them what they need?

7. Make a list of the losses that are weighing on you at this stage of your life. Include such things as physical losses, the close of a chapter in your life, the death of a person close to you, the waning of your youth, etc.

8. How do you usually handle the feelings of grief and frustration when things don't turn out the way you wanted?

9. Imagine that Jesus, through the power and presence of the Holy Spirit, is joining you now on your journey through midlife just as he joined these disciples on the road to Emmaus. What difference does it make to know he is with you?

What do you need from Jesus at this point in your life?

10. Note the chain of events that occurs after Jesus eats with them and leaves (verses 30-35). What changes do you observe in the travelers' attitudes and behavior?

11. How might their experience and testimony have encouraged the other disciples?

What from your own experience with Christ can you share with someone who is going through a hard time of loss?

READ ISAIAH 43:18-19.

12. What does God say here about dealing with the past? What does he say about the future?

Life Changes

☙13. What things from the past do you need to release, entrusting them to God's care? How will you be different once you let go of the things that hold you to the past?

Take time to pray for each other's special needs. Remember that the Spirit of Christ is with you as you walk into the "new things" he has waiting for you.

Freedom in Forgiveness

JOHN 8:1-11; ROMANS 7:19; 8:1-11

Many of us facing the transition of midlife carry deep regrets within our hearts. Some of us have pursued selfish goals and hurt others in the process. Others know the hollowness of making other people our first priority rather than the Lord. Some of us are haunted by the times we have allowed ourselves to be used or abused. Midlife is a good time to take a moral inventory of our lives and let go of the sins of the past.

This scene from John 8 is one of the most tender and touching passages in all of the Gospels, revealing a Savior who feels genuine compassion for sinners. Jesus had the capacity to give mercy and grace in a way that didn't excuse the sin but instead directed people to a new path—and that's good news for all of us.

1. Is it harder for you to forgive or to be forgiven? Why?

READ JOHN 8:1-11.

2. What is the setting for this dramatic scene? Who are the main characters?

3. What is the real motivation fueling the Pharisees' interrogation?

4. As usual, Jesus' response is not what the religious leaders expected. Why do you think Jesus responds as he does (verses 6-8)?

5. Compare and contrast the mood of the crowd at the beginning of this incident and at the end of it. Why the change?

6. If you had been the woman, how would you have felt during this incident? What might be going through your mind?

7. Jesus forgives the woman her terrible sin. What are the conditions of her forgiveness?

How would she have the power to obey Jesus' command in verse 11?

8. Is there any sin God won't forgive? See Luke 12:10.

9. Who leaves this scene unforgiven? Why are those sinners unforgiven?

READ ROMANS 7:19 AND 8:1-11.

10. What does Romans 7:19 say about the dilemma of sin?

11. How does the Holy Spirit help us deal with personal sin?

Life Changes

12. What specific steps can you take to apply and appropriate the awesome grace of Christ in your everyday life?

Midlife is a natural time to make amends where you can and to surrender regrets about your past to God, whose intent is that you live in his grace and mercy. Take time now to pray and ask God to show you how to deal with the sin in your life. If you are holding on to guilt and shame for thirty minutes after you have confessed your sin to him, perhaps you are praying to the wrong god. Think it over!

Starting Over

JOHN 4:1-30; PHILIPPIANS 3:12-14

*M*idlife is often the time we become aware of some of our mixed baggage from the past. We have memories that haunt and hurt as well as memories that bless and enrich our lives. Some of us may feel bound by past mistakes and failures, while others are able to learn from those mistakes and move on. The ways of carrying our past are as varied as our personalities and temperaments.

"When it comes to dealing with my past," one friend told me, "I take the Bible seriously. I am forgetting it. I get to press on!" she exclaimed. She *gets* to press on, to persevere, to start over. Moving ahead is not a burden, but the privilege and calling of every Christian. And we can do so because of the healing, forgiving, grace-giving mercy of Jesus Christ, who comes to us where we are and sets us free to start over, one day at a time.

1. What is one good way you have found to deal with
    your baggage from the past?

READ JOHN 4:1-30.

♍2. Note the details given at the beginning of this story
      (verses 4-8). What do you learn about Jesus? about
      the woman at the well?

♍3. What is unusual about Jesus' taking the initiative to
      talk with this woman (verses 9,27)?

4. This woman carried some pretty heavy baggage from the past (verses 16-18). In what ways might her lifestyle have affected her self-esteem?

5. Why does Jesus seem to change the subject (verses 16-17)?

How does this relate to the woman's request in verse 15?

6. What is your response to the remarkable revelations Jesus makes about himself (verses 13,25-26)?

7. What conclusion does the woman arrive at following her encounter with Jesus (verse 29)?

8. In what ways does Jesus' initiative with the woman at the well enable her to start a new life?

How are others affected by these changes (see verses 28-30,39)?

9. What difference would Jesus' invitation to give him top priority in her affections and worship make in her everyday life?

10. To what people, places, things, substances, or activities have you given the primary love that rightfully belongs to Christ?

What have been the results of misplacing your first love?

Read Philippians 3:12-14.

11. What about the apostle Paul's perspective on the past and the future is significant to you? Why?

12. Think back on your life and consider some of your regrets. What does "pressing on" mean to you at this midpoint of your life?

Life Changes

13. In what areas of your life would you like to make a new and fresh start? What steps can you take this week to begin?

Pray for God's continued guidance and perspective in your life, knowing that he loves you and will meet you where you are—but he also wants to free you to experience a fresh start.

Transformations

JOHN 2:1-11

*T*hroughout his earthly life, Jesus responded to individuals and their needs. He didn't have a "one size fits all" kind of ministry; he didn't do the same work with every person. Instead, our profoundly sensitive and compassionate Savior reached out to meet the exact need of the person before him, transforming brokenness into wholeness, lack into plenty, chaos into calmness, and darkness into light.

In this account of the first recorded miracle that Jesus performed, we see him meeting a seemingly small need by taking something quite common and turning it into something special. Through his Holy Spirit at work today, Jesus is still able to transform the mundane and ordinary aspects of our own lives into creations of significance and beauty.

1. Do you tend to see your life as ordinary or as something special? Why?

Read John 2:1-11.

2. List the characters involved in this drama.

If you had been at the wedding, which character would you like to have been? Why?

3. Why does Mary believe she can trust Jesus with this project?

Why does Jesus resist?

4. What makes Jesus change his mind and move out of his resistance to meet the need of the hour (verse 11)?

5. Why are the servants willing to go along with Jesus' unusual instructions?

What evidence is there (if any) that the servants knew they were helping Jesus perform a miracle?

6. How do people at the wedding respond to this miracle?

7. Make a list of the things in your life that you feel are imperfect and inadequate, things that are ordinary, boring, or irritating to you.

8. Step back from your list and try to be objective about these items. Are you willing to let Jesus, the living Christ, have his way with these aspects of your life that are not quite what you would like them to be? Why or why not?

9. Under what circumstances has Jesus, through the Holy Spirit, turned "water into wine" in the lives of men and women today? Discuss examples you've seen.

◥10. Jesus said, "I came that they may have life, and have it abundantly" (John 10:10, NRSV). What does Jesus mean?

How does Jesus' desire to give you an abundant life affect your attitude toward your present circumstances?

11. Read Romans 8:28. What does this Scripture say about the activity of God in your circumstances today?

Life Changes

◥12. Surrendering our wills to God and cooperating with him are disciplines that must be exercised daily. What will you do to develop the habit of these two powerful acts?

Remember that God is able to transform what we think is emptiness into fullness, and he can work amazing deeds in situations that, to us, seem impossible. The key is surrendering what we have to him and then cooperating with his creative power.

What Do I Have to Give?

LUKE 7:36-50

I have a friend who doesn't believe she has anything worth giving to others. Crippled by self-doubt and self-criticism, she keeps herself bound up in inferiority and self-consciousness, depriving others of her gifts and annoying those who keep reassuring her that, indeed, what she has to give is needed.

Another friend of mine is able to give what she has with joyful abandon. She doesn't concern herself with whether or not her gifts are as polished or exciting as someone else's. She doesn't hamstring herself by worrying about what other people will think. Instead, out of a deep, abiding love for Christ and other people, she exercises her gifts freely and generously.

By midlife all of us have accumulated a wealth of experience and wisdom. Furthermore, each one of us has unique gifts, talents, and abilities to offer to the Lord for his use.

1. Of the two women described above, which is most like you? Explain.

READ LUKE 7:36-50.

2. What is the setting of this story? Who are the main characters and what is the mood of the event?

3. With what attitude does the woman approach Jesus?

4. Summarize the woman's actions in verse 38. What does this gift cost her?

5. How does Jesus react to this overt act of love and affection? Do you think he is embarrassed? What does it cost him to receive this extravagant gift?

6. Perfume was a precious commodity in Jesus' day. In the woman's mind and heart, what do you think her gift to Jesus represents?

In what ways is this woman's gesture the result of an overflowing for Jesus?

7. What is Jesus trying to teach Simon and the others with his parable (verses 41-47)?

8. What are some of your unique talents or gifts? (If you need help, ask someone else to share their observations about your gifts.)

9. What keeps many women from exercising their gifts freely, spontaneously, and unselfconsciously as the woman in this story did?

10. How do you think the woman felt after she had lavishly shown her love and affection for Jesus by giving the precious perfume?

   How do you feel when you give your gifts to Christ by serving others freely and lovingly?

Life Changes

11. What does the woman in this story have to teach midlife women about giving?

12. What gift do you need to offer to the living Christ today?

Think about what God may be challenging you to give to others at this point in your journey—and then give it joyfully. He welcomes the gift you offer to others in his name, just as he welcomed the gift of the woman who anointed his feet.

A New Vision for the Future

EPHESIANS 1:1-14; 3:16-21; PHILIPPIANS 4:8-9;
HEBREWS 12:1-3

The desperate call came in the middle of the afternoon. The bright and energetic woman was a new acquaintance of mine. She had a whole lot going for her, but the difficult challenges of midlife had suddenly caught her by surprise. "I know I'll get through this," she told me, "if I can just catch a spark of hope that what lies ahead of me is good and that God isn't finished with me yet."

How well I understand her fears and feelings. Having made my own journey through the whirlwind of midlife transitions, I know that God will indeed keep on granting new life, new opportunities, and new vistas for those who are faithful to him. His loving and gracious work in us continues through all the stages and passages of life. The good news of the gospel is a message of hope and promise, of possibility and potential, of growth and grace all the days of our lives.

1. What part of your future are you fearful about right now? What are you looking forward to?

READ EPHESIANS 1:1-14.

2. Make a list of all the benefits we have "in Christ" (verse 3).

What practical differences do these benefits make in your life?

3. As believers, what does our future ultimately hold?

4. In what ways do these marvelous truths encourage you as you look toward the future?

READ PHILIPPIANS 4:8-9.

5. Describe some ways this passage challenges you to think differently about your midlife circumstances.

6. How can thinking differently help us to live out the
    truths of the inheritance we have in Christ? Give an
    example or two.

READ HEBREWS 12:1-3.

7. How does looking to Jesus help you face the future
    with hope?

8. What hindrances in your life do you need to set
    aside right now to focus more closely on Jesus?

READ EPHESIANS 3:16-21.

9. According to this prayer, what does God desire for each of us?

10. Do you feel really rooted in God's love? Why or why not?

How can knowing that you are fully loved help you face an unknown future with confidence?

Life Changes

11. Given both the wealth of experience you have
     gained from living and the assurances of God's sus-
     taining grace found in this study of Scripture, what
     encouragement and advice can you give a friend
     who is approaching the midlife years?

12. Think back over the topics we have studied, then
     write out your own midlife prayer to the Lord:
     What are your regrets? fears? What are you thankful
     for? What do you want God to do in and through
     you right now? Write down details of that vision for
     yourself. Remember that you are much loved and
     that God will walk with you into the future.

Leader's Notes

Study 1: Remembering Who Made Me

Question 10. You may want to discuss that midlife offers an opportunity to let go of various responsibilities and attachments as well as to clear out physical and emotional spaces. Praying the different parts of this psalm as their own prayer may help group members recognize those things, both tangible and intangible, they need to release and identify the things they need to embrace.

Study 2: Remembering Who I Am

Question 2. At various times in the history of the Jewish people, God called out prophets—special messengers who spoke to the Jews in his behalf. The prophets always called the people back to a vital relationship with God, which included doing things God's way instead of their own way.

Isaiah, considered one the greatest of all the prophets, lived sometime around 600–700 B.C., and he did most of his writing and speaking in and around Jerusalem. At this time, the nation of Israel was divided into two kingdoms (Judah and Israel) and was led by wicked kings.

Question 4. Isaiah 43:5-6 prophesies of the time when the children of Israel would spend seventy years in exile in Babylonia at the mercy of pagan kings and evil rulers. Throughout Israel's history, the prophets would say, "Return to God!"

They repeated this message over and over was because God had revealed to them the if-then principle: IF Israel chose to rebel against God's ways, THEN they would, by their own actions, leave themselves open to dominance and rule by pagan forces. The if-then principle also works redemptively— and it's functioning in our lives today. If we return to God, then he will bless us. This theme is played throughout Jewish history.

STUDY 3: LETTING GO AND HANDLING LOSS

Question 5. See also John 20:14 and 21:4. Either there was something different about Jesus after his resurrection so his followers did not recognize him or God purposely veiled their eyes.

Question 7. Encourage the group to have the boldness to name their specific losses and to be clear and precise about what comes to an end at midlife. This is an opportunity to admit feelings of grief, confusion and sadness, anger and fear and to confess them to God, who understands.

Question 13. There are things outside of our lives that keep us from experiencing the presence of the living Christ. Those things that are *within,* however, are also blocks to his presence. Fear, guilt, shame, resentment, anger, pride, and a lack of belief that Christ loves you enough to join you on your journey can keep you from knowing Christ's presence in the midst of your life. Sometimes we prefer to hold on to our problems; we become attached to them, clinging to them tenaciously because we prefer to feel bad. We must let go of what is behind in order to be open to what lies ahead!

STUDY 4: FREEDOM IN FORGIVENESS

Question 3. "The law required that both parties to adultery be stoned (Leviticus 20:10; Deuteronomy 22:22). The leaders were using the woman as a trap so they could trick Jesus. If Jesus said the woman should not be stoned, they would accuse him of violating Moses' law. If he urged them to execute her, they would report him to the Romans, who did not permit the Jews to carry out their own executions (John 18:31)"(*Life Application Bible*, Wheaton, Ill.: Tyndale House Publishers, 1991, p. 1892).

Question 8. Luke 12:10 states that blaspheming against the Holy Spirit is the only unforgivable sin. If there's time, you may want to discuss what this verse means, since this can be troubling to many Christians. "The unforgivable sin means attributing to Satan the work that the Holy Spirit accomplishes (see…Matthew 12:31,32; Mark 3:28,29). Thus it is deliberate and ongoing rejection of the Holy Spirit's work and even of God himself" (*Life Application Bible*, p. 1829).

STUDY 5: STARTING OVER

Question 2. Jacob's well was on property that had formerly belonged to the patriarch Jacob. Usually women went twice each day, morning and evening, to draw water. This woman of ill repute went at noon, perhaps to avoid contact with others who might censure her.

Question 3. The Samaritans were so-called half-breeds, one of the reasons pure Jews hated them and would do almost anything to avoid going through Samaria. For Jesus, a Jew, to talk to a Samaritan was quite shocking. For Jesus, a Jewish man, to approach a Samaritan woman with a reputation such as hers was even more outrageous.

Question 5. Jesus used what was common and near at hand to teach this woman about the Living Water that would change her life. How like Jesus to meet her where she was and to communicate with her in a way that she would quickly understand!

Question 8. This woman had given herself away to many other men, seeking love in the only way she knew how. Jesus was able to show her that if she would give to him her worship and love, then she would not need to seek love in all the wrong places.

Her experience with Jesus also changed other people's lives (see verse 39). The woman at the well has been called "the first evangelist" because, having encountered the transforming grace of Jesus, she then rushed to tell her neighbors and friends what Jesus had done for her.

STUDY 6: TRANSFORMATIONS

Question 10. Jesus is talking about more than possessions or a carefree life. He is talking about a deeper joy and a life of *spiritual abundance.* Galatians 5:22-23 offers more insight about the spiritual abundance he gives.

Question 12. Encourage the group to cite the spiritual disciplines that can move us forward in our Christian growth and in the abundant Christian life. These include Bible reading, prayer, meditation, service, corporate worship, giving, etc. Also, it's good to note that God sometimes uses us to influence and encourage one another in this process of surrender and cooperation. You might ask these follow-up questions: "Who has God used to help you grow? In what places might God be calling you to help someone else move forward?"

Study 7: What Do I Have to Give?

Question 8. Every person who has been called into relationship with Jesus Christ has also been called to exercise her own unique gifts in service to God. In addition to natural talents, everyone also has been given spiritual gifts (see Romans 12:3-8).

What Should We Study Next?

*T*o help your group answer that question, we've listed the Fisherman Studyguides by category so you can choose your next study.

TOPICAL STUDIES

Angels by Vinita Hampton Wright

Becoming Women of Purpose by Ruth Haley Barton

Building Your House on the Lord: Marriage and Parenthood by Steve and Dee Brestin

The Creative Heart of God: Living with Imagination by Ruth Goring

Discipleship: The Growing Christian's Lifestyle by James and Martha Reapsome

Doing Justice, Showing Mercy: Christian Actions in Today's World by Vinita Hampton Wright

Encouraging Others: Biblical Models for Caring by Lin Johnson

The End Times: Discovering What the Bible Says by E. Michael Rusten

Examining the Claims of Jesus by Dee Brestin

Friendship: Portraits in God's Family Album by Steve and Dee Brestin

The Fruit of the Spirit: Growing in Christian Character by Stuart Briscoe

Great Doctrines of the Bible by Stephen Board

Great Passages of the Bible by Carol Plueddemann

Great Prayers of the Bible by Carol Plueddemann

Growing Through Life's Challenges by James and Martha Reapsome

Guidance & God's Will by Tom and Joan Stark

Heart Renewal: Finding Spiritual Refreshment by Ruth Goring

Higher Ground: Steps Toward Christian Maturity by Steve and Dee Brestin

Images of Redemption: God's Unfolding Plan Through the Bible by Ruth Van Reken

Integrity: Character from the Inside Out by Ted Engstrom and Robert Larson

Lifestyle Priorities by John White

Marriage: Learning from Couples in Scripture by R. Paul and Gail Stevens

Miracles by Robbie Castleman

One Body, One Spirit: Building Relationships in the Church by Dale and Sandy Larsen

The Parables of Jesus by Gladys Hunt

Parenting with Purpose and Grace by Alice Fryling

Prayer: Discovering What the Bible Says by Timothy Jones and Jill Zook-Jones

The Prophets: God's Truth Tellers by Vinita Hampton Wright

Proverbs and Parables: God's Wisdom for Living by Dee Brestin

Satisfying Work: Christian Living from Nine to Five by R. Paul Stevens and Gerry Schoberg

Senior Saints: Growing Older in God's Family by James and Martha Reapsome

The Sermon on the Mount: The God Who Understands Me
by Gladys Hunt

Spiritual Gifts by Karen Dockrey

Spiritual Hunger: Filling Your Deepest Longings by Jim and
Carol Plueddemann

A Spiritual Legacy: Faith for the Next Generation by Chuck
and Winnie Christensen

Spiritual Warfare by A. Scott Moreau

The Ten Commandments: God's Rules for Living by Stuart
Briscoe

Ultimate Hope for Changing Times by Dale and Sandy
Larsen

Who Is God? by David P. Seemuth

Who Is Jesus? In His Own Words by Ruth Van Reken

Who Is the Holy Spirit? by Barbara Knuckles and Ruth Van
Reken

Wisdom for Today's Woman: Insights from Esther by Poppy
Smith

Witnesses to All the World: God's Heart for the Nations
by Jim and Carol Plueddemann

Women at Midlife: Embracing the Challenges by Jeanie
Miley

Worship: Discovering What Scripture Says by Larry Sibley

BIBLE BOOK STUDIES

Genesis: Walking with God by Margaret Fromer and
Sharrel Keyes

Exodus: God Our Deliverer by Dale and Sandy Larsen

Ezra and Nehemiah: A Time to Rebuild by James Reapsome

(For Esther, see Topical Studies, *Wisdom for Today's Woman*)
Job: Trusting Through Trials by Ron Klug
Psalms: A Guide to Prayer and Praise by Ron Klug
Proverbs: Wisdom That Works by Vinita Hampton Wright
Ecclesiastes: A Time for Everything by Stephen Board
Jeremiah: The Man and His Message by James Reapsome
Jonah, Habakkuk, and Malachi: Living Responsibly
      by Margaret Fromer and Sharrel Keyes
Matthew: People of the Kingdom by Larry Sibley
Mark: God in Action by Chuck and Winnie Christensen
Luke: Following Jesus by Sharrel Keyes
John: The Living Word by Whitney Kuniholm
Acts 1–12: God Moves in the Early Church by Chuck and
      Winnie Christensen
Acts 13–28, see *Paul* under Character Studies
Romans: The Christian Story by James Reapsome
1 Corinthians: Problems and Solutions in a Growing Church
      by Charles and Ann Hummel
Strengthened to Serve: 2 Corinthians by Jim and Carol
      Plueddemann
Galatians, Titus, and Philemon: Freedom in Christ
      by Whitney Kuniholm
Ephesians: Living in God's Household by Robert Baylis
Philippians: God's Guide to Joy by Ron Klug
Colossians: Focus on Christ by Luci Shaw
Letters to the Thessalonians by Margaret Fromer and Sharrel
      Keyes
Letters to Timothy: Discipleship in Action by Margaret
      Fromer and Sharrel Keyes
Hebrews: Foundations for Faith by Gladys Hunt
James: Faith in Action by Chuck and Winnie Christensen

1 and 2 Peter, Jude: Called for a Purpose by Steve and Dee
    Brestin

How Should a Christian Live? 1, 2, and 3 John by Dee
    Brestin

Revelation: The Lamb Who Is a Lion by Gladys Hunt

BIBLE CHARACTER STUDIES

Abraham: Model of Faith by James Reapsome

David: Man After God's Own Heart by Robbie Castleman

Elijah: Obedience in a Threatening World by Robbie
    Castleman

Great People of the Bible by Carol Plueddemann

King David: Trusting God for a Lifetime by Robbie
    Castleman

Men Like Us: Ordinary Men, Extraordinary God by Paul
    Heidebrecht and Ted Scheuermann

Moses: Encountering God by Greg Asimakoupoulos

Paul: Thirteenth Apostle (Acts 13–28) by Chuck and
    Winnie Christensen

Women Like Us: Wisdom for Today's Issues by Ruth Haley
    Barton

Women Who Achieved for God by Winnie Christensen

Women Who Believed God by Winnie Christensen

Printed in the United States
by Baker & Taylor Publisher Services